VIOLIN

MOTOWN CLASSICS

T0081990

HOW TO USE THE CD ACCOMPANIMENT:

A MELODY CUE APPEARS ON THE RIGHT CHANNEL ONLY.
IF YOUR CD PLAYER HAS A BALANCE ADJUSTMENT, YOU CAN ADJUST THE VOLUME
OF THE MELODY BY TURNING DOWN THE RIGHT CHANNEL.

THE CD IS PLAYABLE ON ANY CD PLAYER, AND IS ALSO ENHANCED SO MAC AND PC USERS
CAN ADJUST THE RECORDING TO ANY TEMPO WITHOUT CHANGING THE PITCH!

ISBN: 978-1-4584-0563-0

HAL•LEONARD®
CORPORATION
7777 W. BLUEMOUND RD. P.O. BOX 13819 MILWAUKEE, WI 53213

Visit Hal Leonard Online at
www.halleonard.com

CONTENTS

◆ ABC

VIOLIN

Words and Music by ALPHONSO MIZELL,
FREDERICK PERREN, DEKE RICHARDS
and BERRY GORDY

❖ ② AIN'T NO MOUNTAIN HIGH ENOUGH

VIOLIN

Words and Music by NICKOLAS ASHFORD
and VALERIE SIMPSON

❸ BABY LOVE

VIOLIN

Words and Music by BRIAN HOLLAND,
EDWARD HOLLAND and LAMONT DOZIER

◆ ENDLESS LOVE

VIOLIN

Words and Music by
LIONEL RICHIE

◆ HOW SWEET IT IS
(To Be Loved by You)

VIOLIN

Words and Music by EDWARD HOLLAND,
LAMONT DOZIER and BRIAN HOLLAND

◆ I CAN'T HELP MYSELF

(Sugar Pie, Honey Bunch)

VIOLIN

Words and Music by BRIAN HOLLAND,
LAMONT DOZIER and EDWARD HOLLAND

❼ I JUST CALLED TO SAY I LOVE YOU

VIOLIN

Words and Music by
STEVIE WONDER

◆8 I'LL BE THERE

VIOLIN

Words and Music by BERRY GORDY,
HAL DAVIS, WILLIE HUTCH
and BOB WEST

◆ ❾ MY CHERIE AMOUR

Violin

Words and Music by STEVIE WONDER,
SYLVIA MOY and HENRY COSBY

THREE TIMES A LADY

VIOLIN

Words and Music by
LIONEL RICHIE

◆ MY GIRL

VIOLIN

Words and Music by WILLIAM "SMOKEY" ROBINSON
and RONALD WHITE

19

◆12 STOP! IN THE NAME OF LOVE

VIOLIN

Words and Music by LAMONT DOZIER,
BRIAN HOLLAND and EDWARD HOLLAND

❸ THE TRACKS OF MY TEARS

VIOLIN

Words and Music by WILLIAM "SMOKEY" ROBINSON,
WARREN MOORE and MARVIN TARPLIN

WHAT'S GOING ON

Violin

Words and Music by RENALDO BENSON,
ALFRED CLEVELAND and MARVIN GAYE

◆15 YOU'VE REALLY GOT A HOLD ON ME

VIOLIN

Words and Music by
WILLIAM "SMOKEY" ROBINSON